HO-HO-HO-LARIOUS CHRISTMAS JOKES FOR KIDS

by

MERRY MARY E. HIRSCH

Published in the United States by
Mary E. Hirsch

contact@swellthoughts.com

First Edition

Other Joke Books by
Mary E. Hirsch

April Fool's Fun
The Joke Is On Ewe

This book is for Vicky and Devin

And Dasher and Dancer and
Prancer and Vixen and Comet and
Cupid and Donner and Blitzen
and, of course, Rudolph and
Olive.

How do fire fighters put out a burning Christmas tree?

> With a fire ho-ho-hose.

What kind of gymnastics do elves like to perform?

> Christmas card-wheels.

Where do you find Santa's helpers at the library?

> In the elf-help section.

What part of the body do you only see during Christmas?

Mistletoe.

What do you call someone who doesn't believe in Santa?

A rebel without a Claus.

What do you call a scary reindeer?

A cariboo.

Why does Santa have three gardens?

So he can ho ho ho.

Knock Knock.
Who's there?
Carol
Carol who?
Carolers are singing, can't you hear us.

What do you call a bad puppy on Christmas?

Felix Naughty Dog.

What do snowmen eat for breakfast?
Ice Crispies.

Beware of SANTA JAWS

Why did the elves ask the turkey to join the band?

Because he had the drum sticks.

Knock Knock
Who's there?
Wayne
Wayne who?
Wayne in a manger...!

What did one snowman say to the other snowman?

Do you smell carrots?

Where did the mistletoe go to become famous?

Holly-wood.

What did Santa use to walk when he sprained his ankle?

A candy cane.

Why did Linda put oatmeal in the elm tree and the maple tree?

She wanted to have porridge in a pair of trees.

Why did Eric put a Christmas tree in this bedroom?

His mom told him to spruce it up.

Where do you find the smartest Christmas plants?

In the Ivy League.

What do you call it when Santa slips on a roof?

Snow fall.

What Christmas song is hidden in this alphabet:
"A B C D E F G H I J K M N O P Q R S T U V W X Y Z"?

Noel (No "L")

Knock Knock
Who's there?
Snow
Snow who?
Snow use I've forgotten my name!

Why did Sally give her grandma two hives?

She said she wanted two bee home for Christmas.

What do you call an elf who sings?

A wrapper!

What do you call Santa living at the South Pole?

A lost clause.

Knock Knock
Who's there?
Chris!
Chris who?
Christmas!!!!

What nationality is Santa Claus?

North Polish.

Where does Santa and his reindeer go to get hot chocolate?

Star-bucks.

Knock Knock.
Who's there?
Rudolph
Rudolph who?
Rudolph you not
to let me in.

How much did Santa pay for his sleigh?

Nothing, it was on the house.

Where does Santa sleep when he's traveling?

In a Ho, Ho, Hotel.

Rudolph the Red: "It's going to rain."
Mrs. Red: "How do you know?"
Rudolph the Red: "Because Rudolph the Red knows rain, dear."

Knock Knock
Who's there?
Holly
Holly who?
Holly Days are here

Ho-ho-ho-larious Christmas Jokes

Frosty's Word Search
Find the pictured words.
They are either down or across.

snowflake   tree   Santa   fireplace

```
O U X T A W Z K Q R X R S A R
A W O S Z C U Q T L G B E V G
M I T T E N S V U L G H Z V Q
T N F I R E P L A C E A X V V
H X R X O G Q V C S C T G B C
Q P D S U H B Y A N J A I N N
Y G W A A I I Y H O A S N V Y
O K C N F G T O A W D F X J L
V B J T R U J M W F U B Y E Q
Q S B A Y A N A J L A L R V C
S T I L E I Z E L A Z I T D A
S H S X C K X Z I K T O Y Z N
T Y D L T R E E F E L I M N D
A J R C F I T K Y C V C P H L
R U R S D V O L T X O Z C U E
```

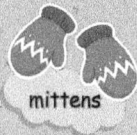

candle   hat   star   mittens

Answers on page 75

Why did Rudolph give Santa a smart phone for Christmas?

So he could take elfies.

Why did Santa get a ticket on Christmas Eve?

He left his sleigh in a snow parking zone.

What did the Christmas tree say to the ornament?

Do you get tired of hanging around?

Why are there no Dairy Queen's at the North Pole?

Santa doesn't want any blizzards.

Knock Knock
Who's there?
Oakham
Oakham who?
Oakham all ye faithful...!

What do you call unmarried chimes?

Single bells.

Why is Lester the Elf always goofing around in the workshop?

He's a snowoff.

What do you call an expensive snowman?

Costly the Snowman.

Why does Santa Claus go down the chimney on Christmas Eve?

Because it soots him.

How does an elf get to Santa's workshop?

By icicle.

Where does Santa keep his money?

A snow bank.

Why did Pat put arrows on the Christmas wreath?

Because it already had a bow.

Why was the ornament addicted to Christmas?

He was hooked on trees.

What do you get when you cross an archer with a gift-wrapper?

Ribbon hood.

How does Santa sing the alphabet?

A B C D E F G...H I J K L M N Oh!,
Oh!, Oh! P Q R S T U V W X Y Z!

Fran: What did the reindeer say to the
football player?
Steve: I don't know.
Fran: "Your Blitzen days are over!"

What kind of ball doesn't bounce?

A snowball.

What do snowmen
eat for breakfast?

Frosted Flakes.

What is a good Christmas meal?

Angel hair pasta.

Knock Knock
Who's there?
Donut
Donut who?
Donut open until Christmas!

Why were the camels so thirsty by the time they got to Bethlehem?

No well (Noel).

SUNDAY MONDAY
TUESDAY WEDNESDAY
THURSDAY FRIDAY
SATURDAY

HAPPY
HOLLER-DAYS

Why do you hang your socks on the fireplace?

Because the dog gets mad if you hang them on him.

Why did Connie throw her salad out the window?

She heard her mom say lettuce snow.

Why are Christmas trees so fond of the past?

Because the present's beneath them.

Knock Knock
Who's there?
Rudolph
Rudolph who?
Money is the Rudolph of all evil!

What do you call people who are afraid of Santa Claus?

Claustrophobic.

What do you call a sheep who doesn't like Christmas?

Baaaaaaaa humbug.

What do you call the wrapping paper leftover from opening presents?

A ChristMESS.

What do you call a snowman that can walk?

Snow-mobile.

Knock Knock
Who's there?
Miss L
Miss L who?
Miss L Toe

What do you get when you combine a
Christmas tree with an iPad?

A pineapple.

Lisa: What does
Santa say at the
start of a race?
Joni: I don't know.
Lisa: "Ready, set,
Ho! Ho! Ho!"

How do sheep say "Merry Christmas"?

"Fleece Navidad."

What's Santa's favorite sandwich?

Peanut butter and jolly.

What do you have in December that you don't have in any other month?

The letter D.

What is the best thing to put into Santa's boots?

Santa's feet.

Why does Santa play hockey?

He wants to check his list – twice.

Why were the wise men chasing Dwayne "The Rock" Johnson?

They were following a star.

What do you call three Ebenezers in one room?

The three Scrooges.

What do you call a Santa with no money?

Saint-NICKEL-LESS.

What do the elves cook with in the kitchen?

Utinsel.

What did the little elves have to do when they got home from school?

Gnome-work.

Knock Knock
Who's there?
Irish
Irish who?
Irish you a Merry Christmas!

What do hip hop artists do on Christmas?

Unwrap.

What did Adam say on the day before
Christmas?

   "It's Christmas, Eve."

Why does Scrooge love all of the reindeer?

   Because every buck is dear to him.

Terry: When is a good time for Santa to
come down the chimney?
Bill: When?
Terry: Anytime!

What's red and white, red and white, red and white?

Santa Claus rolling down the hill.

Who lives at the North Pole, makes toys and rides around in a pumpkin?

Cinder-elf-a.

What do you get if you cross mistletoe and a duck?

A Christmas Quacker.

What is Count Dracula's favorite Christmas story?

> The fright before Christmas.

What do you get when you cross a bell with a skunk?

> Jingle smells.

Why did Dasher carry a suitcase?

> He is a deer-to-deer salesman.

Annie: Did you know Santa had only eight reindeer last Christmas?
Curt: Huh?
Annie: Comet stayed home to clean the sink.

erte __ __ __ __

wsoannm __ __ __ __ __ __ __

ockoie __ __ __ __ __ __

evesl __ __ __ __ __ __

rermy __ __ __ __ __

dre __ __ __

nrgee __ __ __ __ __

ellbs __ __ __ __ __

hrtaiscms __ __ __ __ __ __ __ __ __

rohnt leop __ __ __ __ __ __ __ __ __

ndererei __ __ __ __ __ __ __ __

natas lcusa __ __ __ __ __ __ __ __ __ __

ihegsl __ __ __ __ __ __ __

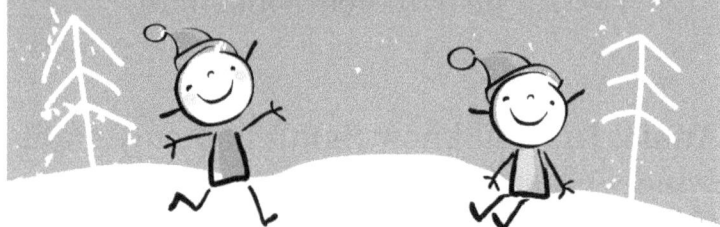

Christmas Word Scramble

Answers on page 74

Connect the dots and
give this angel her wings.

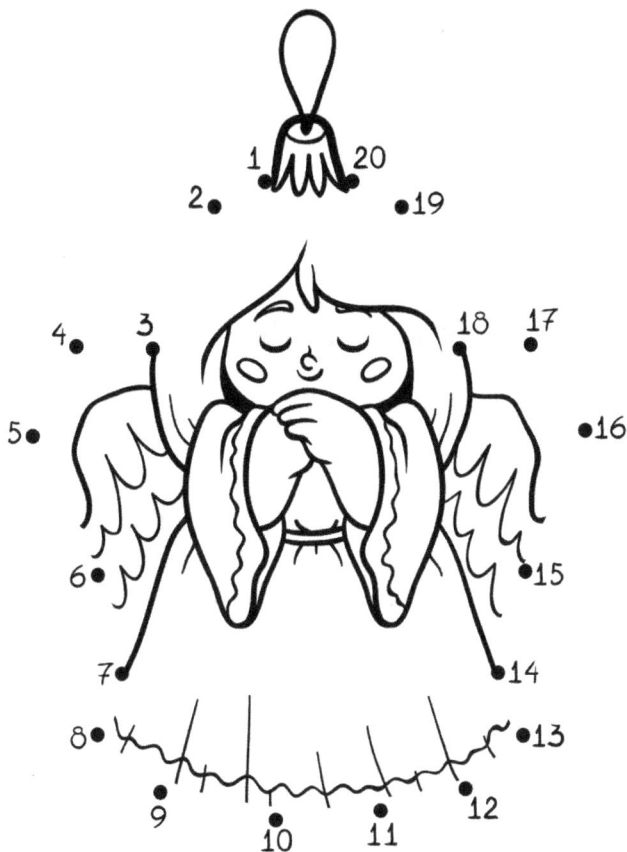

What is Santa's favorite snack food?

Kris Pringles.

When is Santa's favorite season of year?

The fallalalalalalala.

Why does Santa wear black boots?

Because black socks would get all wet.

What's the difference between Santa Claus and a knight?

One slays the dragon and the other drags the sleigh.

Where do lawn ornaments go over winter break?

Gnome for the holidays.

Knock Knock
Who's there?
Yule
Yule who?
Yule be sorry if you don't hurry up and
open this door.

What do you get if you eat Christmas decorations?

Tinselitis.

What do you call a boring Christmas flame?

A candull.

What did the Christmas tree say to the Christmas lights?

"You think you're really bright don't you?"

What did the head elf say at the end of Christmas season?

That's a wrap.

Santa: Jimmy have you been naughty or
nice?
Jimmy: Yes
Santa: Yes? Which is it naughty or nice?
Jimmy: Whichever will get me the most
presents.

Why did Santa hire Rocky to work in gift
wrap?

He's a good boxer.

Who delivers Christmas presents to dogs?

Santa paws.

What did the cow say on Christmas
morning?

Mooooooey Christmas.

What Christmas decoration is the most polite?

> The bows of holly.

What kind of bug hates Christmas?

> A humbug.

Britta: What do snowmen like to do on the weekend?
James: What?
Britta: Chill out.

What do you call Santa when he stops moving?

> Santa Pause.

When does a reindeer have a trunk?

> When he goes on vacation.

What do you get if you cross Santa with an owl?

I don't know but it says Who Who Who.

Knock Knock
Who's there?
Hope
Hope who?
Hope you had a nice holiday!

Why can't you trust baked goods during the holidays?

It might be a pumpkin spy.

Why doesn't the Rope family ever get presents from Santa?

Because they are always knotty not nice.

What do you call a frog hanging from a ceiling?

Mistletoad.

Who doesn't eat on Christmas?

A turkey because it is always stuffed.

Amy: Mark, why did you send me a comedian for Christmas?
Mark: You said you wanted a Christmas card.

Who is Santa's favorite singer?

A-wreatha Franklin.

What is the favorite dance of elves?

They like to limbo under the North Pole.

Why did the elves take Christmas candles to the Smithsonian?

They wanted to make it a wax museum.

What sport do gift wrappers like best?

Bow-ling

Why did the Wise Man ask the Halloween monster for advice?

He needed some Frankin sense.

Help Santa get to Blitzen

Answer on page 76

Coloring Page

Here are some snowglobes that
need you to make them beautiful

How do reindeer stay healthy?

> They take a vitamin chill every day

What did the snowman eat?

> Icebergs with chilli sauce.

What cars do elves drive?

> A toy-ota.

John: How come you never hear anything about the 10th reindeer "Olive"?
Rose: Olive ?
John: Yeah, you know, "Olive the other reindeer, used to laugh and call him names."

Why do mummies like
Christmas so much?

Because of all the
wrapping.

Knock Knock!
Who's there?
Mary and Abby!
Mary and Abby who?
Mary Christmas and a
Abby new year.

Brett: What does Jack Frost like best
about school?
Gertrude: What?
Brett: Snow and tell.

What goes "oh, oh, oh"?

Santa walking backwards.

Why did the baker bring a snowman to the bakery?

He needed to put Frosty on the cake.

Why did Debbie bring her Aunt Joyce to school every day in December?

She wanted to re-Joyce.

What do you get when you cross a funny ballerina with a duck and a Christmas cookie?

A nutty quacker sweet

Why did Janny put a sweater a jacket a hat and a shirt on top of the Gingerbread House?

She was four clothesing on it.

What do monkeys sing at Christmas?

Jungle bells.

Why did Santa cross the road?

To deliver the presents.

Who does Santa call to make repairs on his suit?
He always has Jack Frost clipping at his clothes.

What do you call cutting down a Christmas tree?

Christmas Chopping.

Knock Knock
Who's there?
Orange
Orange who?
Orange you glad you were good all year?

What do you get when you cross a snowman with a vampire?

Frostbite.

Why did Frosty the Snowman want a divorce?

Because he thought his wife was a flake.

What do you call Luke Skywalker in front of his Christmas tree?

The Jedi knight before Christmas.

What did the pine tree say to the plastic tree?

You are such a faker.

What kind of jewelry does an elf give his girlfriend?

A jingle bell rock.

Knock Knock
Who's there?
Tissue.
Tissue Who?
All I Want For Christmas Tissue...

What do you call a Christmas present you will get tomorrow?

A Christmas future.

What do you have if you step on Rudolph's foot?

A paindeer.

Why was Santa shivering at the kitchen table?

> He was eating chili.

What is green and white and red all over?

> A sunburned elf.

What is red and white and green all over?

> A pickle dressed like Santa.

What's invisible and smells like cookies and milk?

> Santa's burps.

Knock Knock
Who's there?
Yule
Yule who?
Yule have fun during the holidays!

Why do you have to put your Christmas tree in a tree stand?

Because trees don't have legs silly.

What do you call it when an elf falls off the Christmas train?
He's off his jolly trolly.

What do you learn at Santa's Helpers school?

The elf-a-bet.

Billy: Is our Christmas tree a pine tree?
Mom: Fir sure.

Why are green and red the colors for
Christmas?

Because red, white & blue were
already taken.

What's the difference between the
Christmas alphabet and the ordinary
alphabet?

The Christmas alphabet has Noel.

What's black, white and red all over?

Santa Claus after he comes down the chimney!

Knock Knock
Who's there?
Avery
Avery who?
Avery merry Christmas!

What did the gingerbread man put on his bed?

A cookie sheet.

What Christmas Carol is a favorite of parents?

Silent Night.

What do you call a can that has the Christmas spirit?

A Merry can.

Why was Santa's little helper depressed?

Because he had low elf esteem.

What do you call Frosty the Snowman in July?

A puddle!

Nancy: Why won't you let Fred and I ride with you on your sled?
Myron: It's a toboggan.
Nancy: So what?
Myron: Then it would be a threeboggan.

Knock Knock
Who's there?
Noel.
Noel Who?
Noelevator in this building I'll have to take the steps

What happened when Elton Elf put the firewood down the garbage disposal?

They had to unlog the drain.

What do snowmen eat for breakfast?

Frosted Flakes.

What happens when you exercise a lot on Christmas?

You become a Christmas sweat-er.

What do you call an elf wearing ear muffs?

Anything you want. He can't hear you.

What comes at the end of Christmas Day?

Y.

Knock. Knock.
Who's there?
Hanna.
Hanna who?
Hanna partridge in a pear tree.

Why does Santa use reindeer to pull his sleigh?

Because moose can't fly.

Mildred: What are you going to give your little brother for Christmas this year?
Perry: I haven't decided yet.
Mildred: What did you give him last year?
Perry: The flu.

What do you call an incomplete Christmas sentence?

A Santa pause

T'was the night before Christmas and all through the house,

Not a creature was stirring, not even a mouse.

The stockings were hung by the chimney with care,

And a note that said: Santa, please don't leave underwear.

What do you call a snowman party?

A Snowball.

Knock Knock
Who's there?
Donut
Donut who?
Donut open til Christmas!

Why did Santa put a clock in his sleigh?

Because he wanted to see time fly.

Who is Santa's favorite rock and roll singer?

Buddy Holly.

Malcolm: Hey Frosty do you want some hot chocolate?
Frosty: Snow Way.

Mary: My dog Freckles always knows where Santa is on Christmas Eve.
Daisy: I don't believe you. Show me.
Mary: Okay Freckles, where is Santa? Where is Santa?
Freckles: Roof, Roof.

After Christmas, what is Santa's favorite holiday?

Falalalalather's Day.

Never catch snowflakes on your tongue until all
the birds have gone south for the winter!

Follow the string to see what letter goes in the box.

Answer on page 77

Knock Knock!
Who's there?
Dexter.
Dexter, who?
Dexter halls with boughs of holly.

What do you call a person doing holiday baking for the first time?

A Christmas cookie rookie.

What do you call an obnoxious reindeer?

RUDEolph.

What do you call a Christmas joke that isn't funny?

The first no-LOL.

What do you call a singing elf with sideburns?

Elfis.

What did Santa say when he got stuck?

Ho Ho Helllpppppp.

Mrs. Claus: "Is it rain or hail?"
Santa: "It's reindeer."

Where do reindeer go to dance?

Christmas balls.

Teacher: Geri, define claustrophobia.
Geri: Fear of Santa Claus?

Why is it so cold at Christmas?

Because it's Decembrrrrr.

What did the Christmas lights say to the Christmas tree?

"We like to hang around you."

What movie do the elves like to watch at Christmas?

Ho-Ho-Home Alone.

Name a child's favorite Christmas king?

A stocking.

Knock Knock
Who's there?
Rabbit.
Rabbit who?
Rabbit up carefully, it's a present!

Why did the dieter go to Bethlehem?

She heard there was a weigh-in the manger.

Who do you call if your presents are stolen?

The Police Navidad.

Why do people put marshmallows in their hot chocolate?

Because they taste horrible in soup.

Knock Knock.
Who's there?
Olive.
Olive, who?
Olive the other reindeer.

Why wouldn't Silly Sam drink his apple cider in the house?

It made him feel like an out cider.

Knock Knock.
Who's there?
Eddie.
Eddie, who?
Eddie or not here comes Christmas.

Where did the kids go when they couldn't find their snowman?

Frost and found.

What's red, white and blue at Christmas time?

A sad candy cane.

What's a big as Santa but weighs nothing?

Santa's shadow.

Why did the gingerbread man go to the doctor?

Because he was feeling crummy.

Darth Vader: I know what you're getting for Christmas.
Luke: How do you know?
Darth Vader: I can feel your presents.

What did Mary Poppins want from Santa?

    Supercalifragilisticexpialisnowshoes.

What is the most popular Christmas carol in the desert?

    Camel ye Faithful.

What did the salt say to the pepper?

    Seasoning Greetings.

Where do the reindeer eat their morning meal?

    At the breakfast stable.

What did Mickey give Minnie for Christmas?

    A Christmouse card.

Where would you find chili beans?

At the North Pole.

Knock Knock
Who's there?
Snow
Snow who?
Snow business like show business!

How do you know Santa Claus is good at karate?

He has a black belt.

What did Santa say after he got spun around and around?

Joy to the Whirled.

What do you call a dozen sticky holiday donuts?

The 12 glaze of Christmas.

Why does Santa go to the doctor right before Christmas Eve?

To get a shingles shot.

Who does Santa take with him to play putt-putt?

Rugolf the Red Nosed Caddy.

Why did the geologists go to the North Pole?

They were looking for jingle bell rocks.

What is Frosty's favorite movie?

Frozen.

ANSWERS TO GAMES

Tree

Bells

Snowman

Christmas

Cookie

North Pole

Elves

Reindeer

Merry

Santa Claus

Red

Sleigh

Green

Word Scramble Answers

```
O U X T A W Z K Q R X R S A R
A W O S Z C U Q T L G B E V G
M I T T E N S V U L G H Z V Q
T N F I R E P L A C E A X V V
H X R X O G Q V C S C T G B C
Q P D S U H B Y A N J A I N N
Y G W A A I I Y H O A S N V Y
O K C N F G T O A W D F X J L
V B J T R U J M W F U B Y E Q
Q S B A Y A N A J L A L R V C
S T I L E I Z E L A Z I T D A
S H S X C K X Z I K T O Y Z N
T Y D L T R E E F E L I M N D
A J R C F I T K Y C V C P H L
R U R S D V O L T X O Z C U E
```

Word Search Answers

Help Santa get to Blitzen

Answer

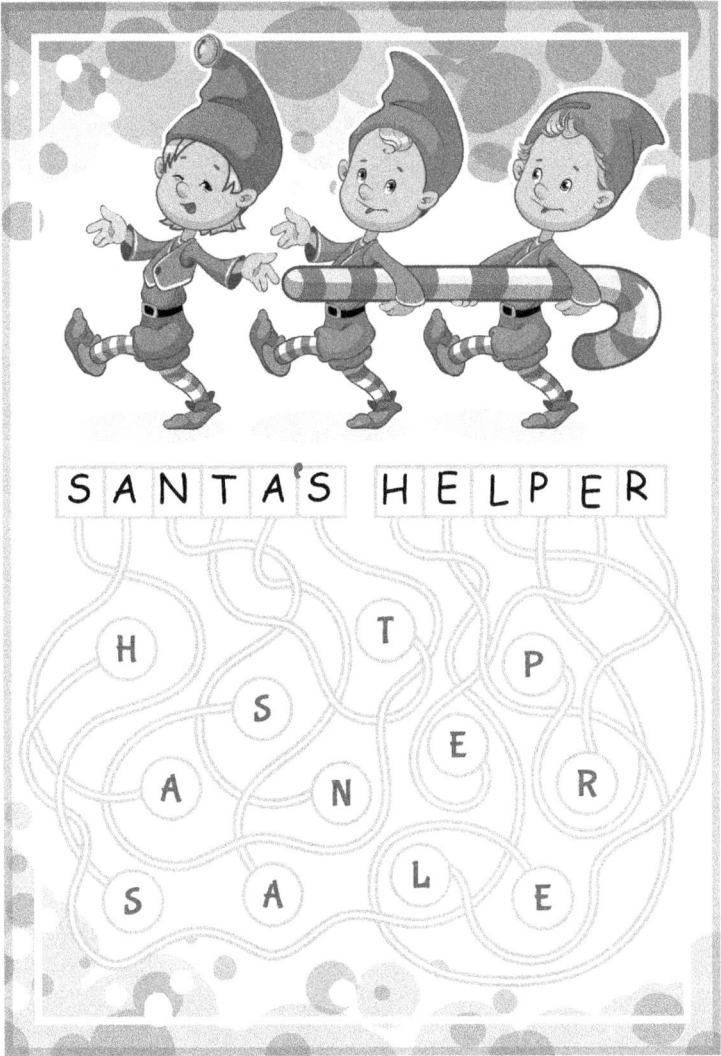

S A N T A'S H E L P E R

Marching Elves Answer

Knock Knock.
Who's there?
Murray.
Murray who?
Murray Christmas to all and
to all a good night.